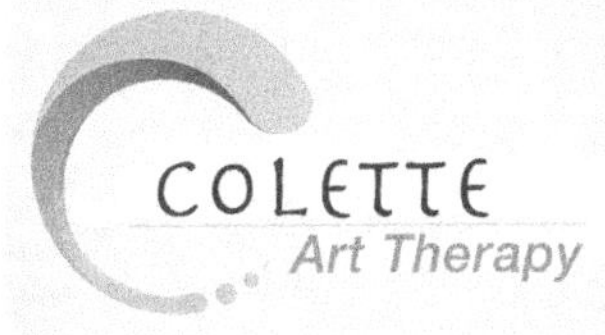

Babies and Flowers

"A Baby is
for a short period of time
In your arms,
but for a lifetime
In your heart.

This is worth more
than silver or gold,
A feeling money
can not buy
and a memory
no one can steal"

*May this book
bring your joy
- Colette*

**Please like our face book page
Colette Art Therapy**

*This book can also be personalised
with photos of family and friends.
See our website for more information.*

www.ColetteArtTherapy.com

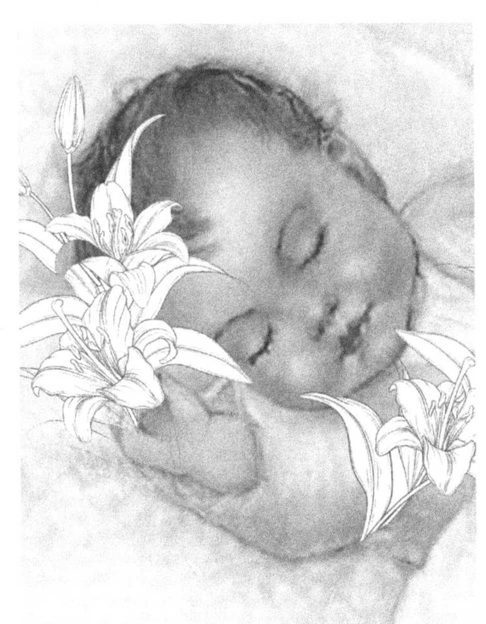

Copyright © 2020. Published by **Treasure_my_Art**

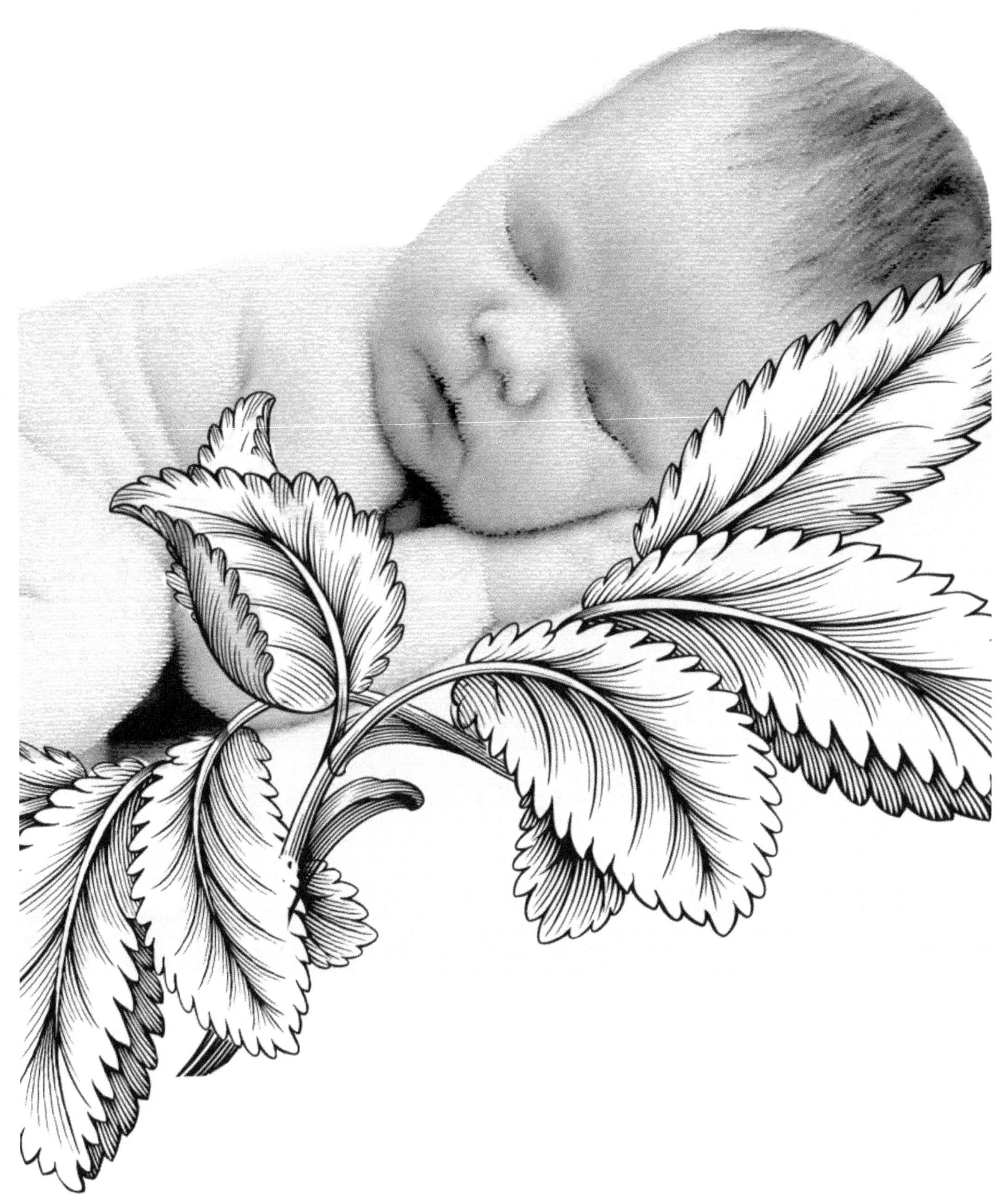

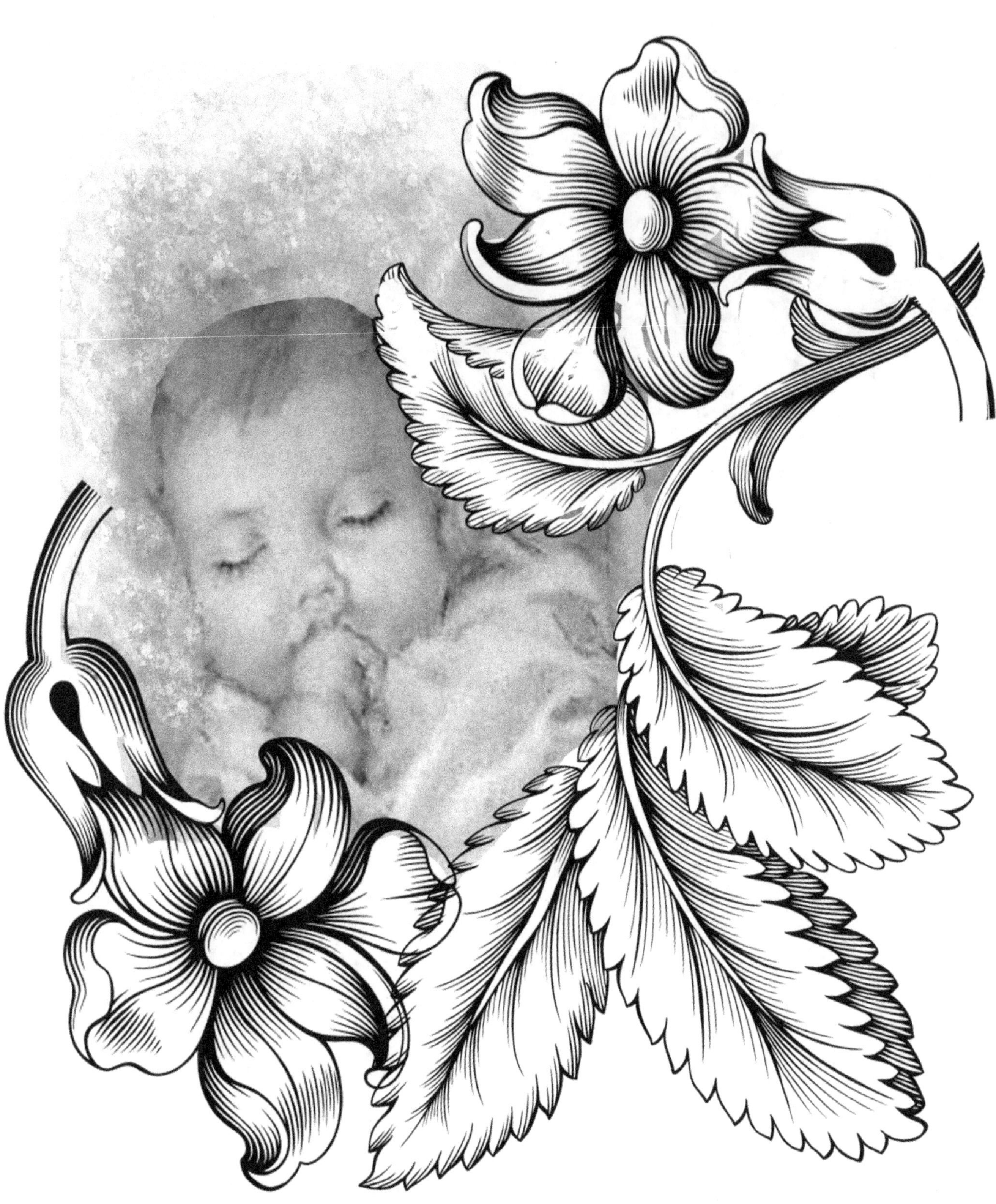

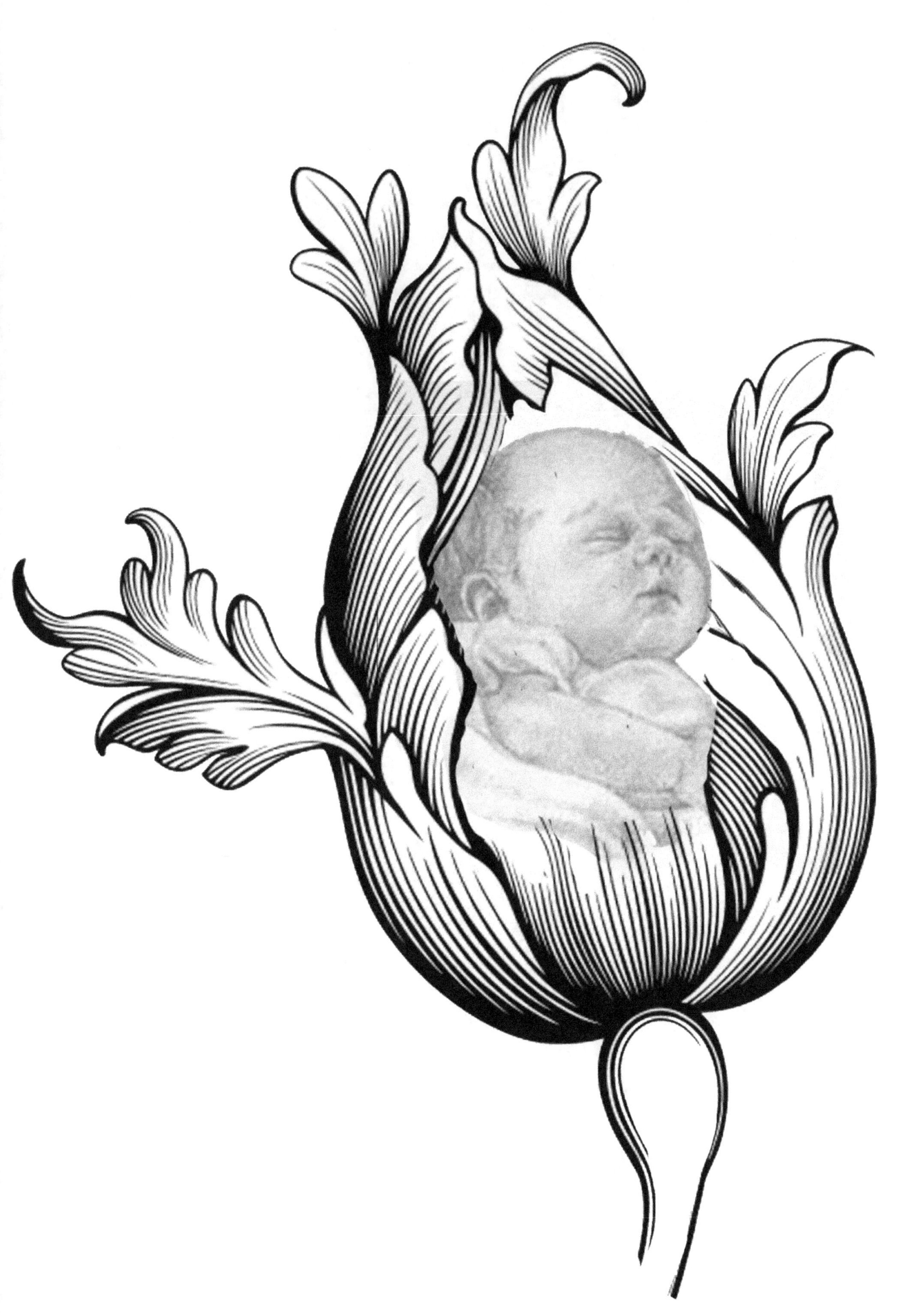

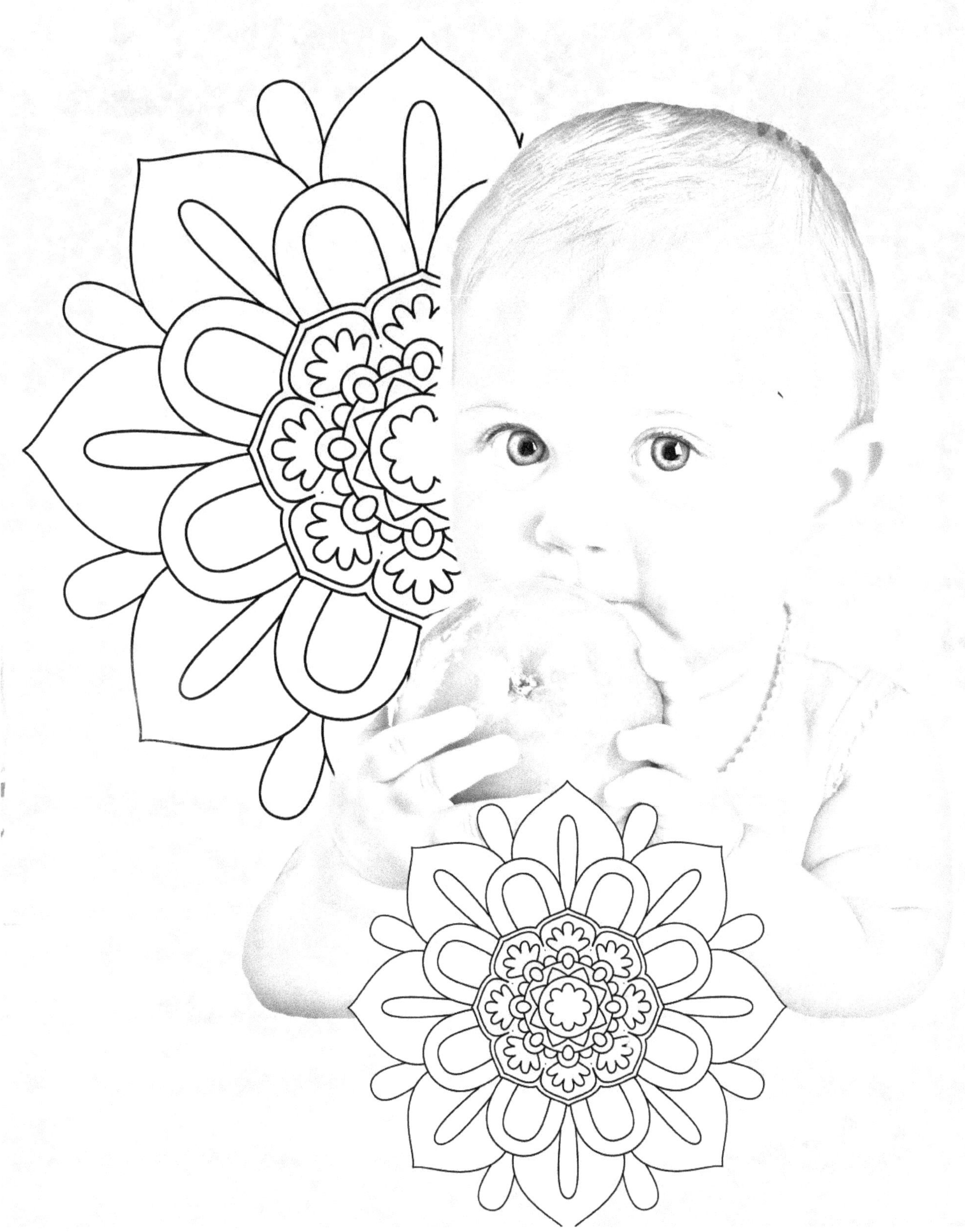

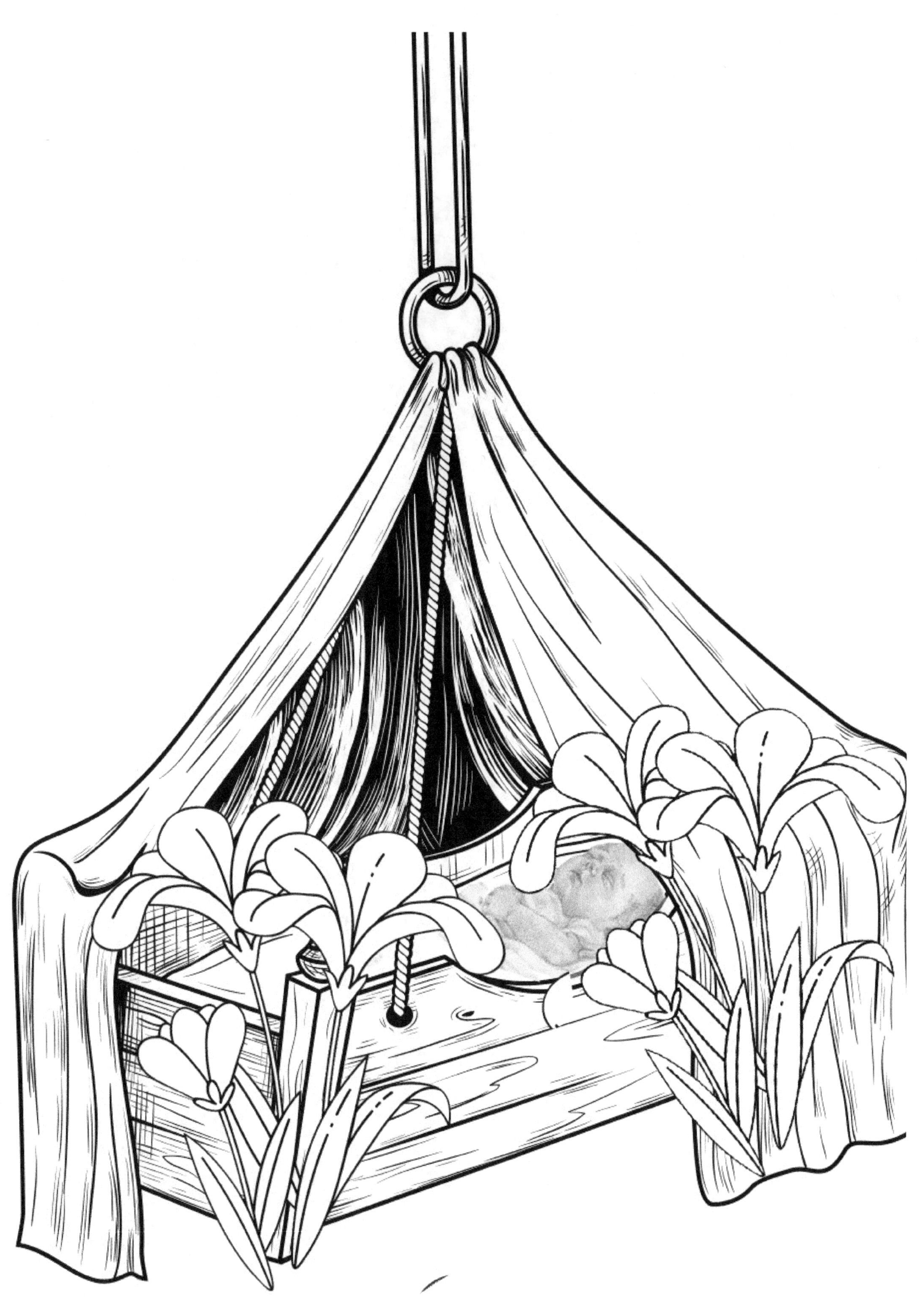

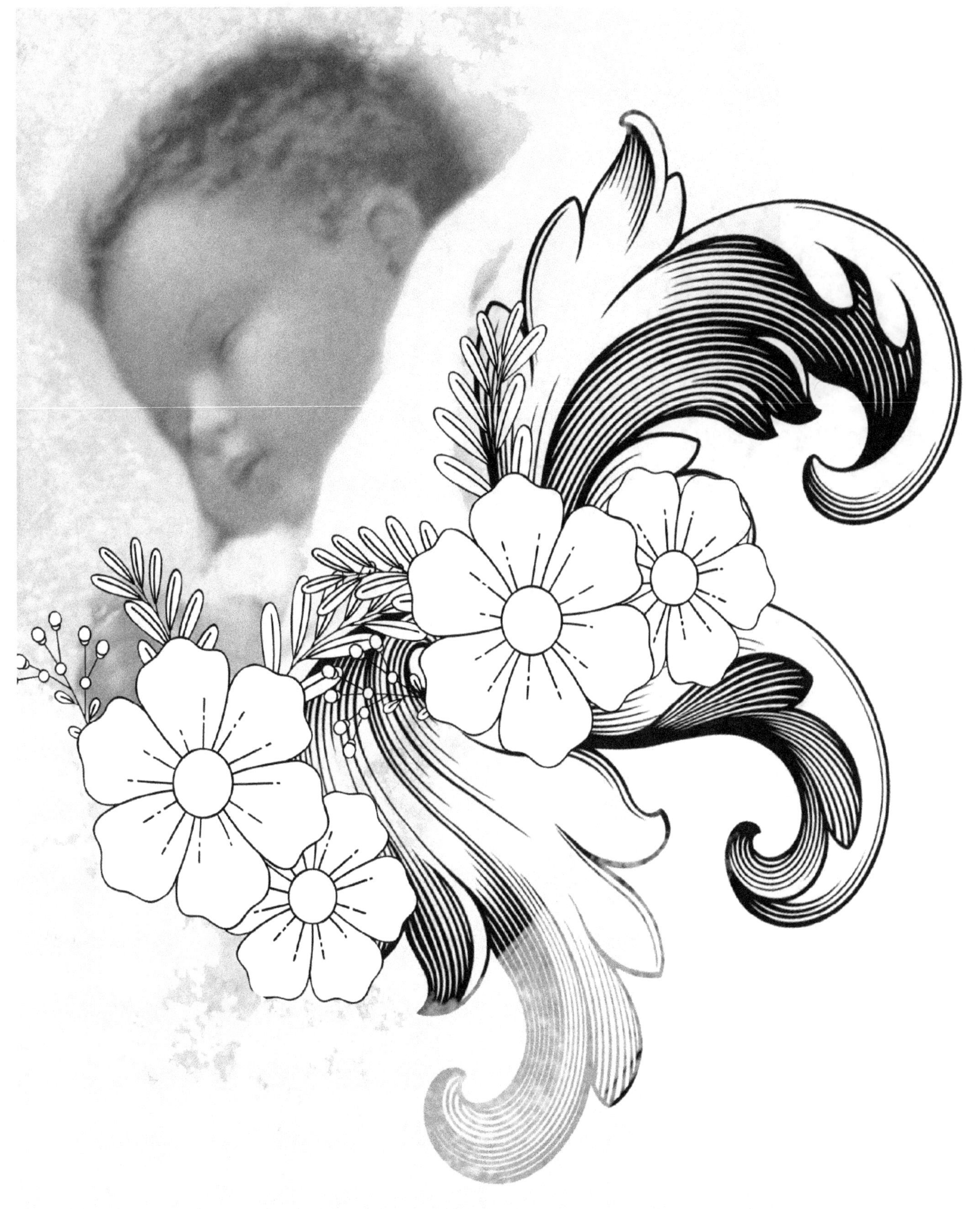

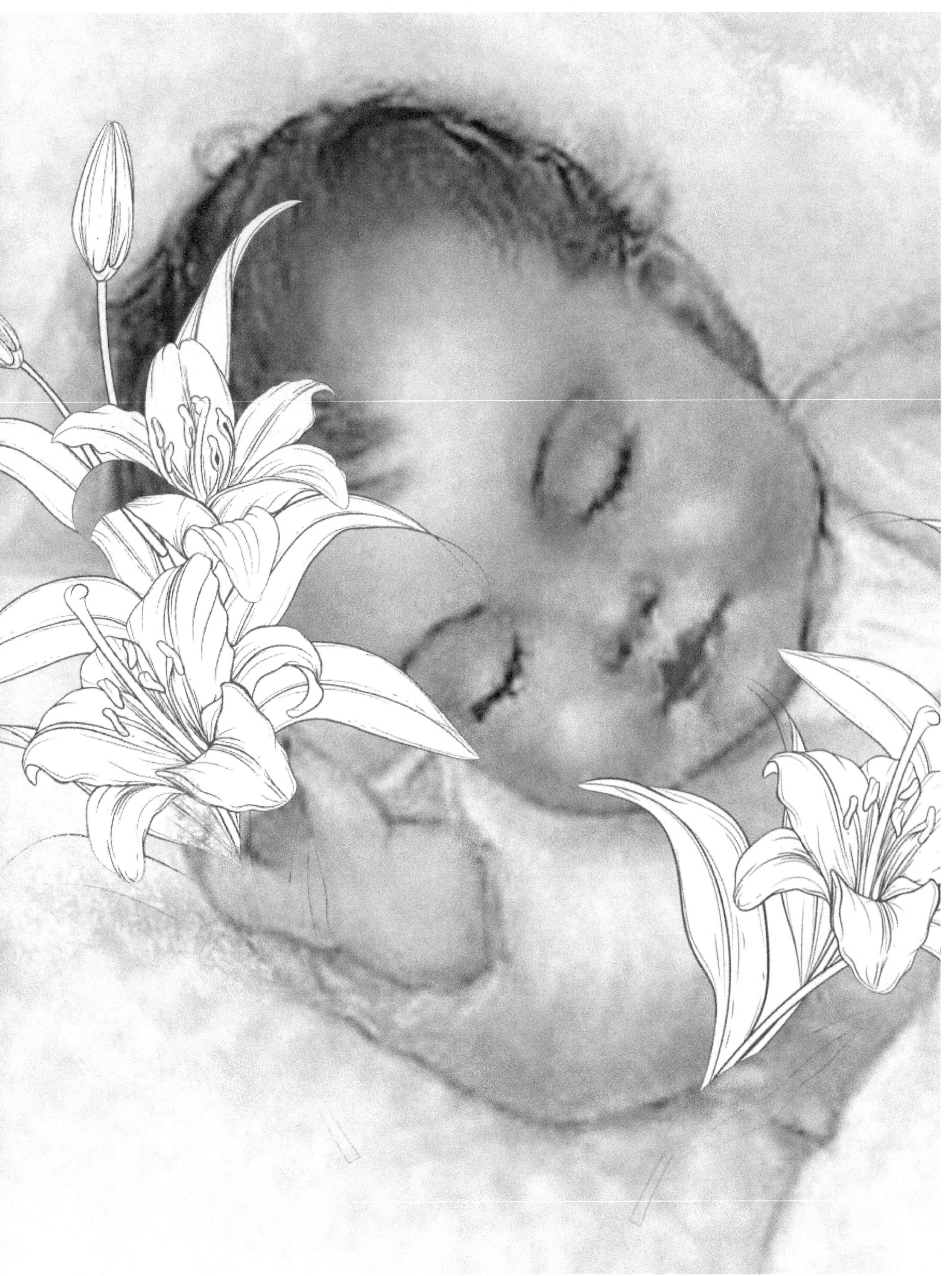

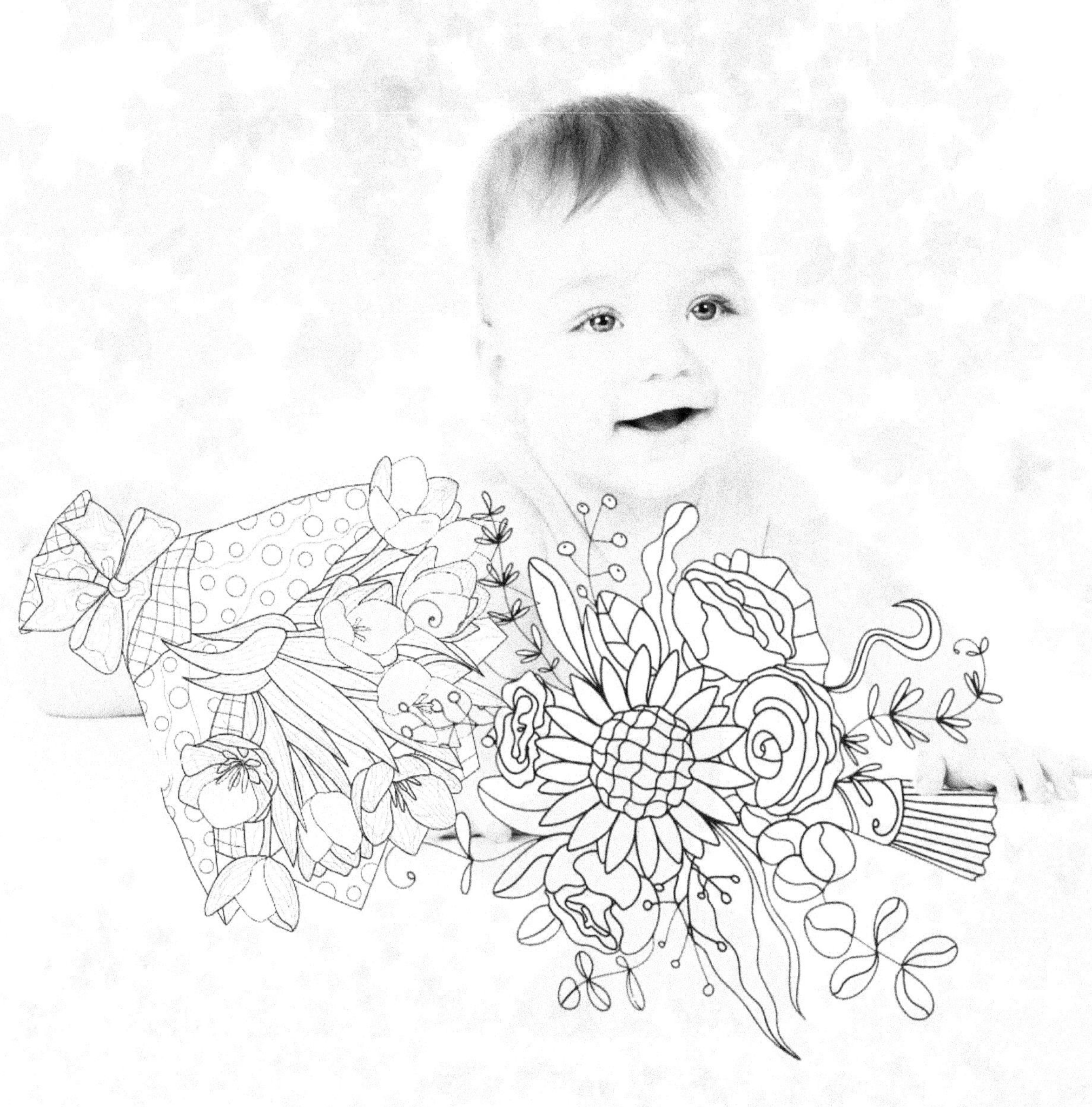

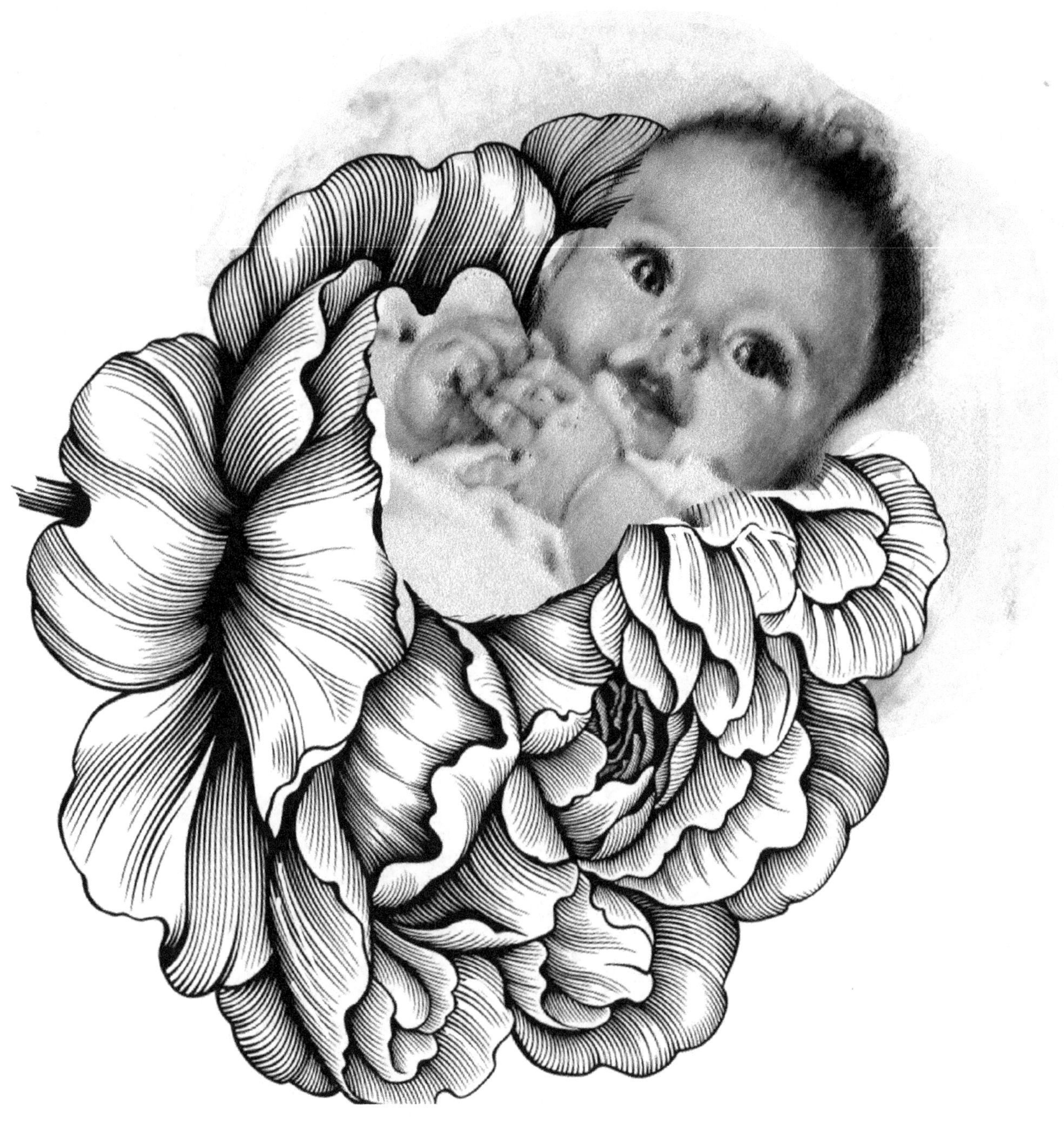

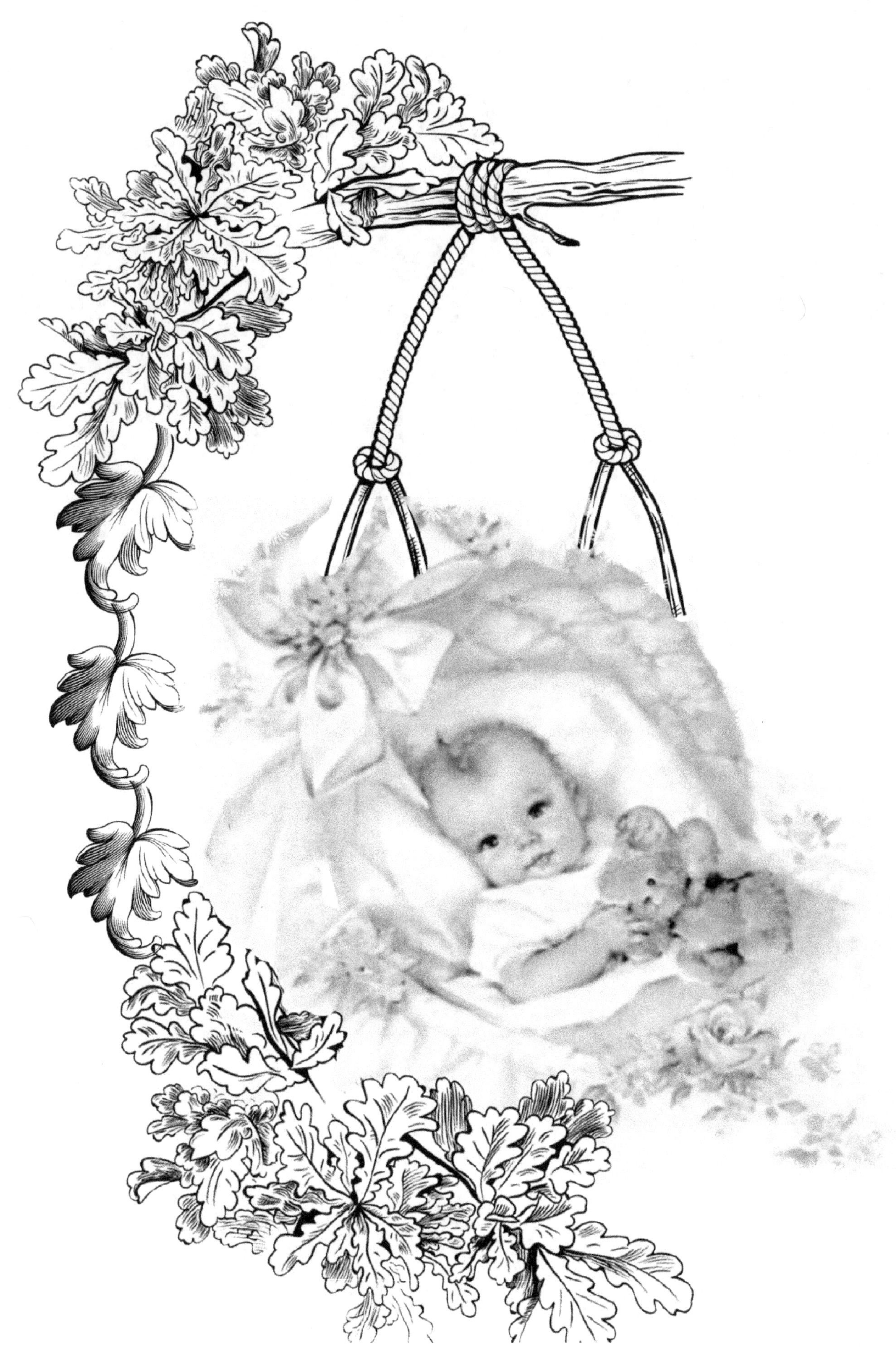

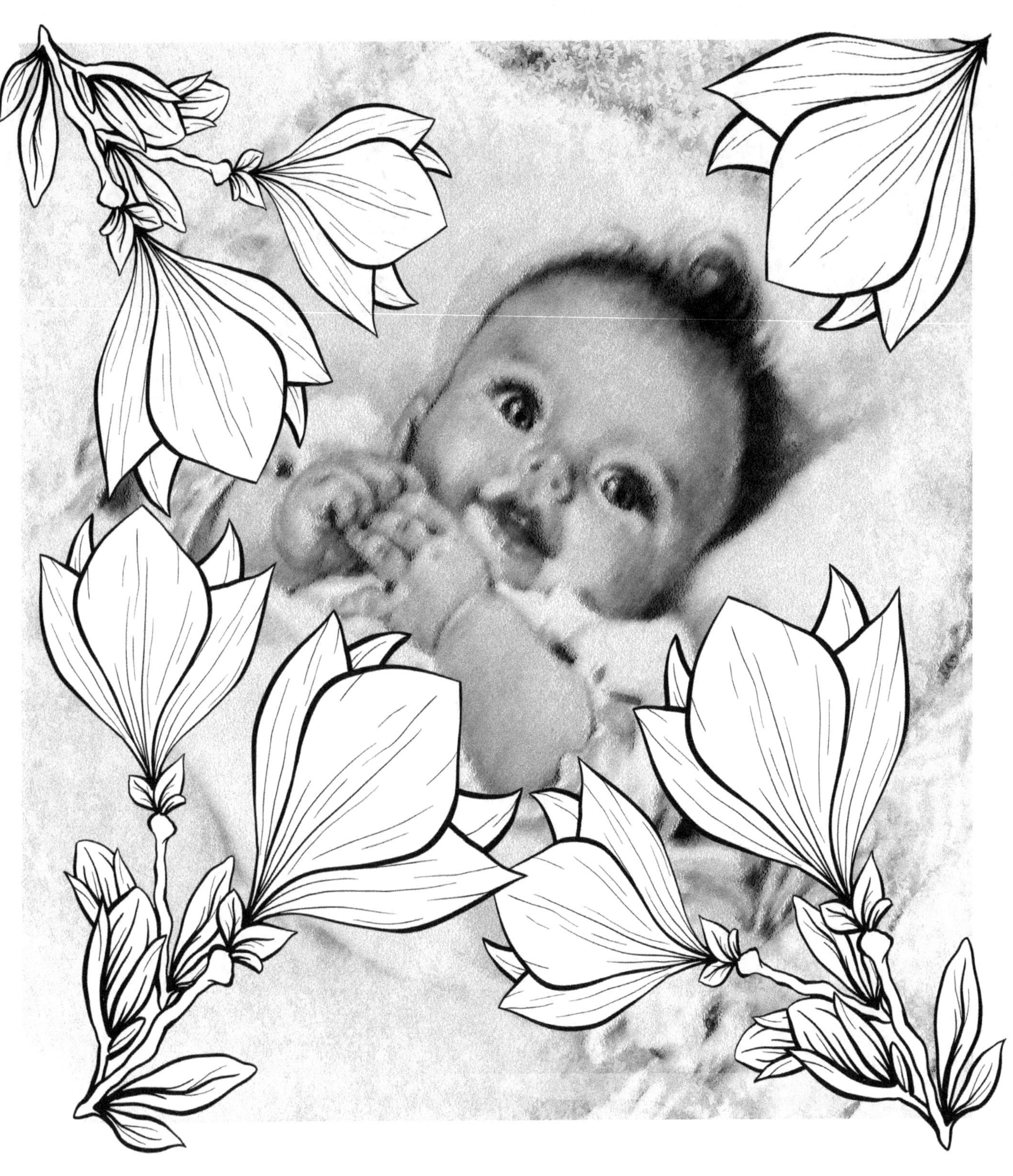

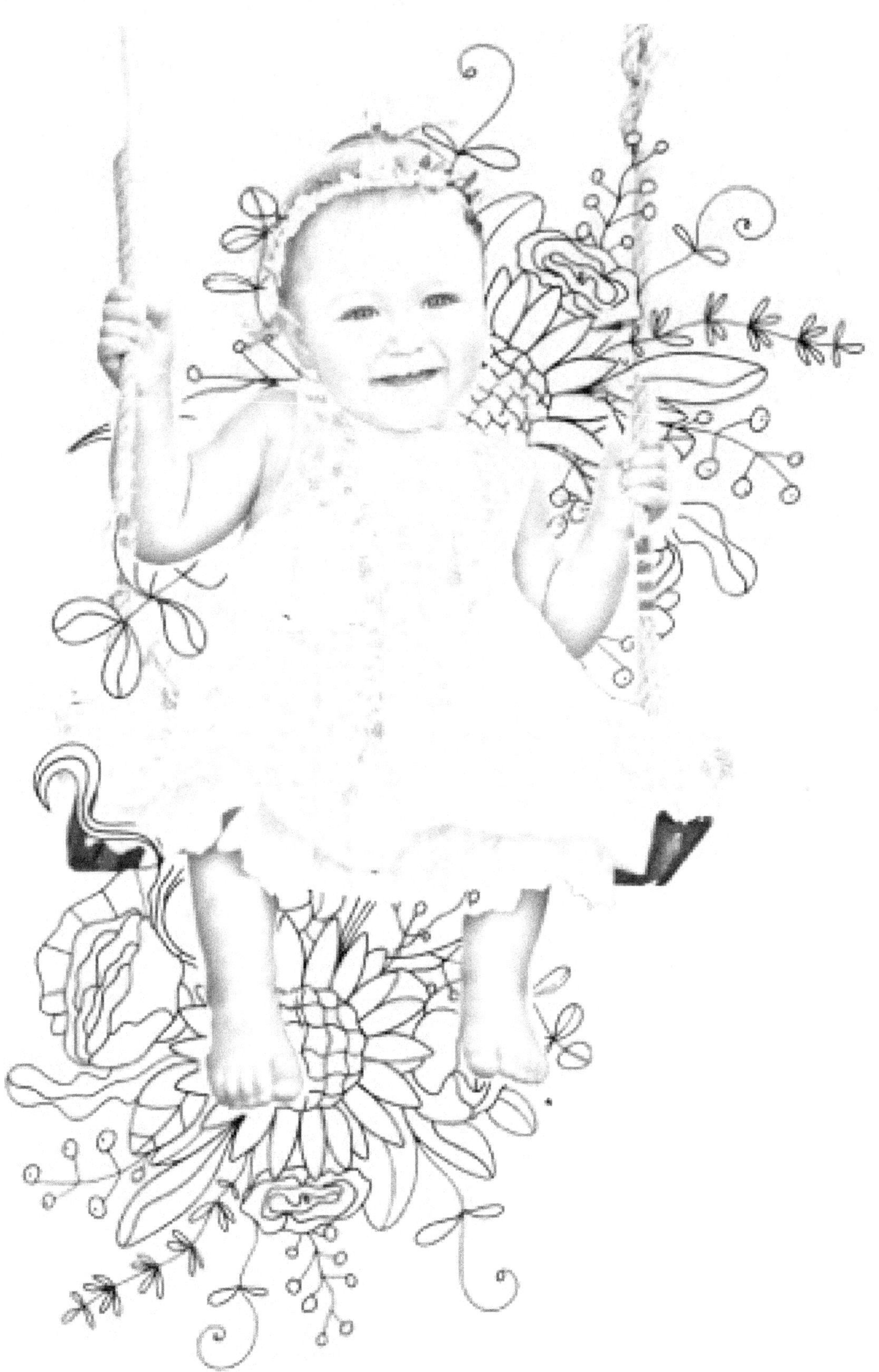

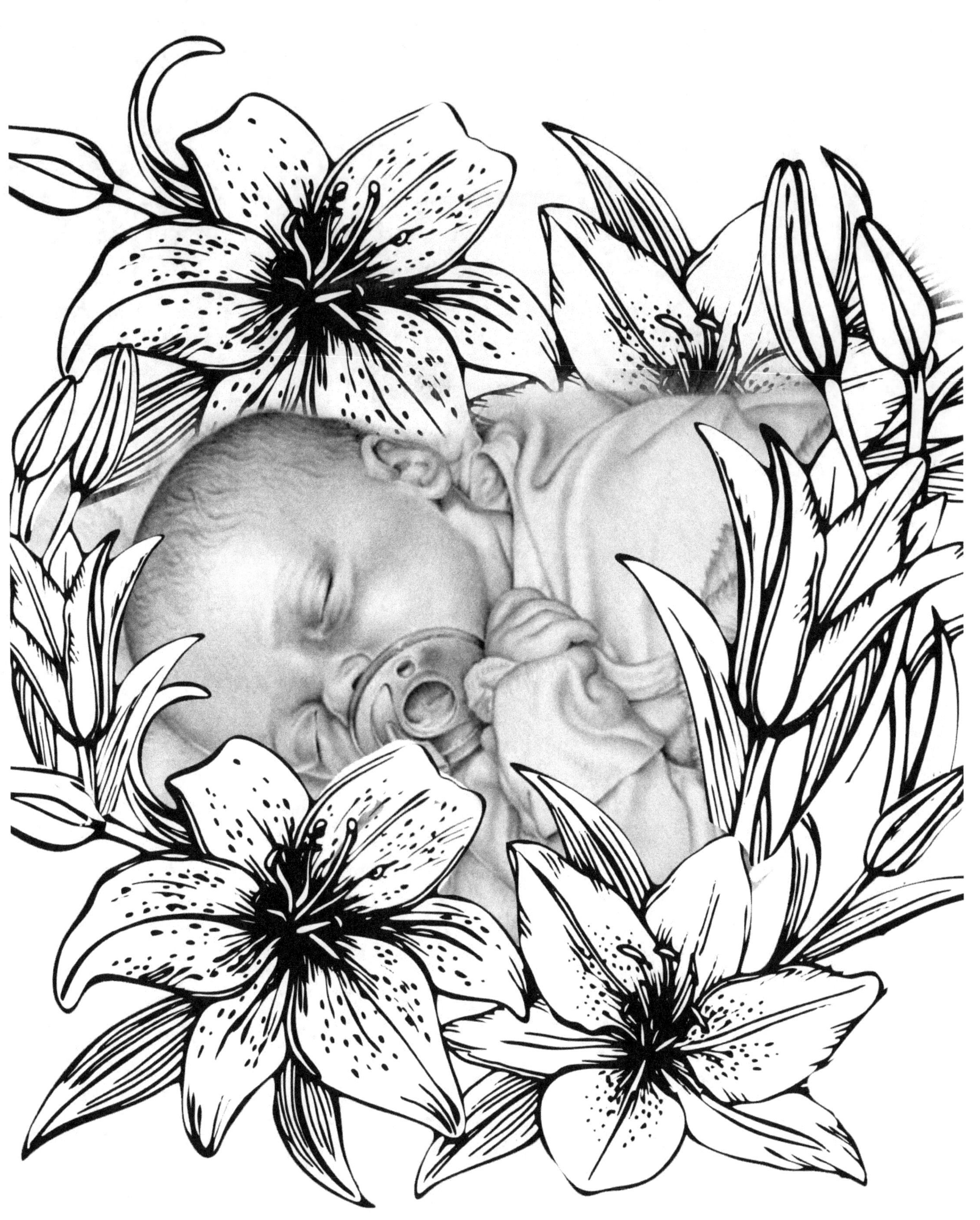

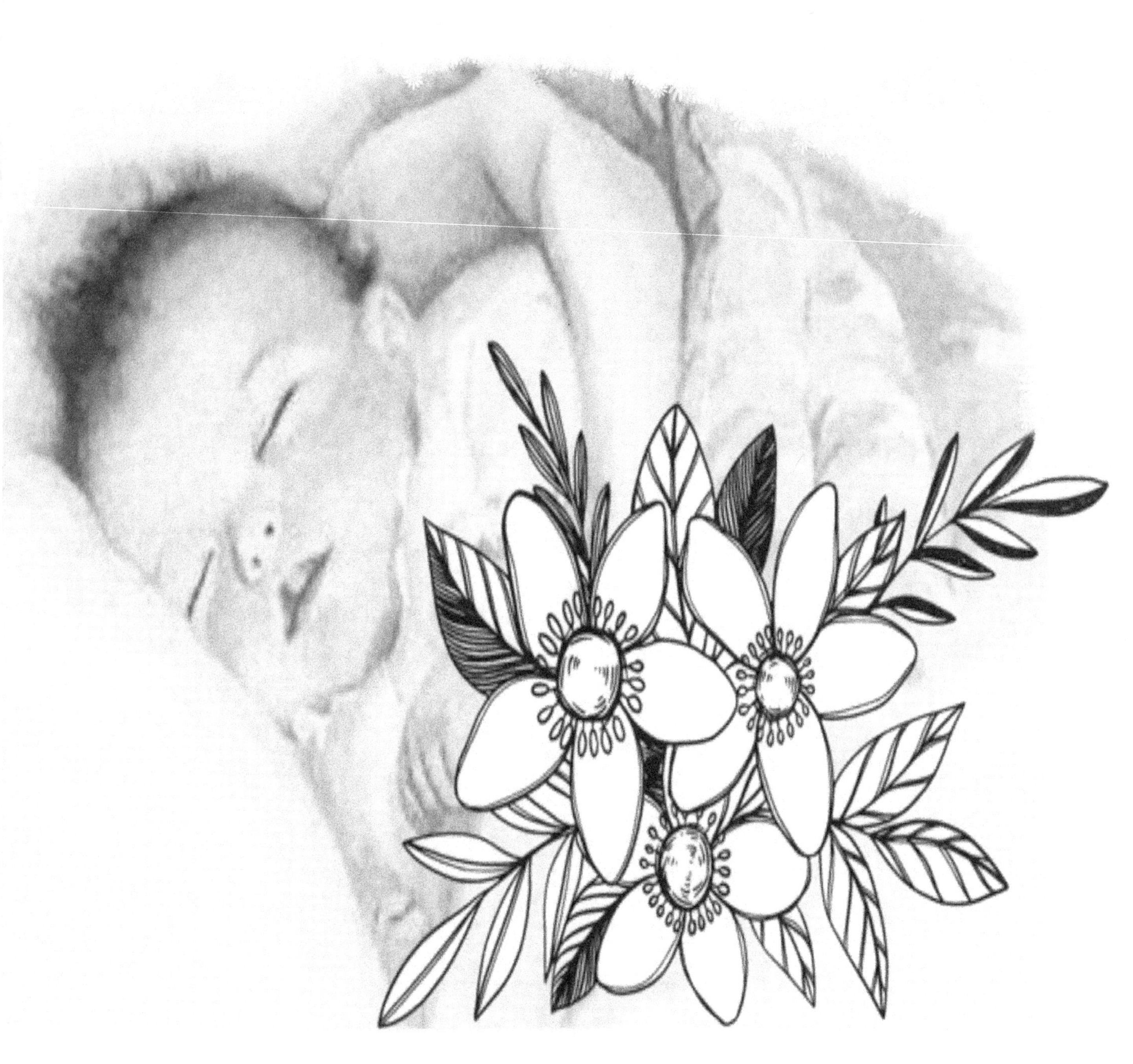

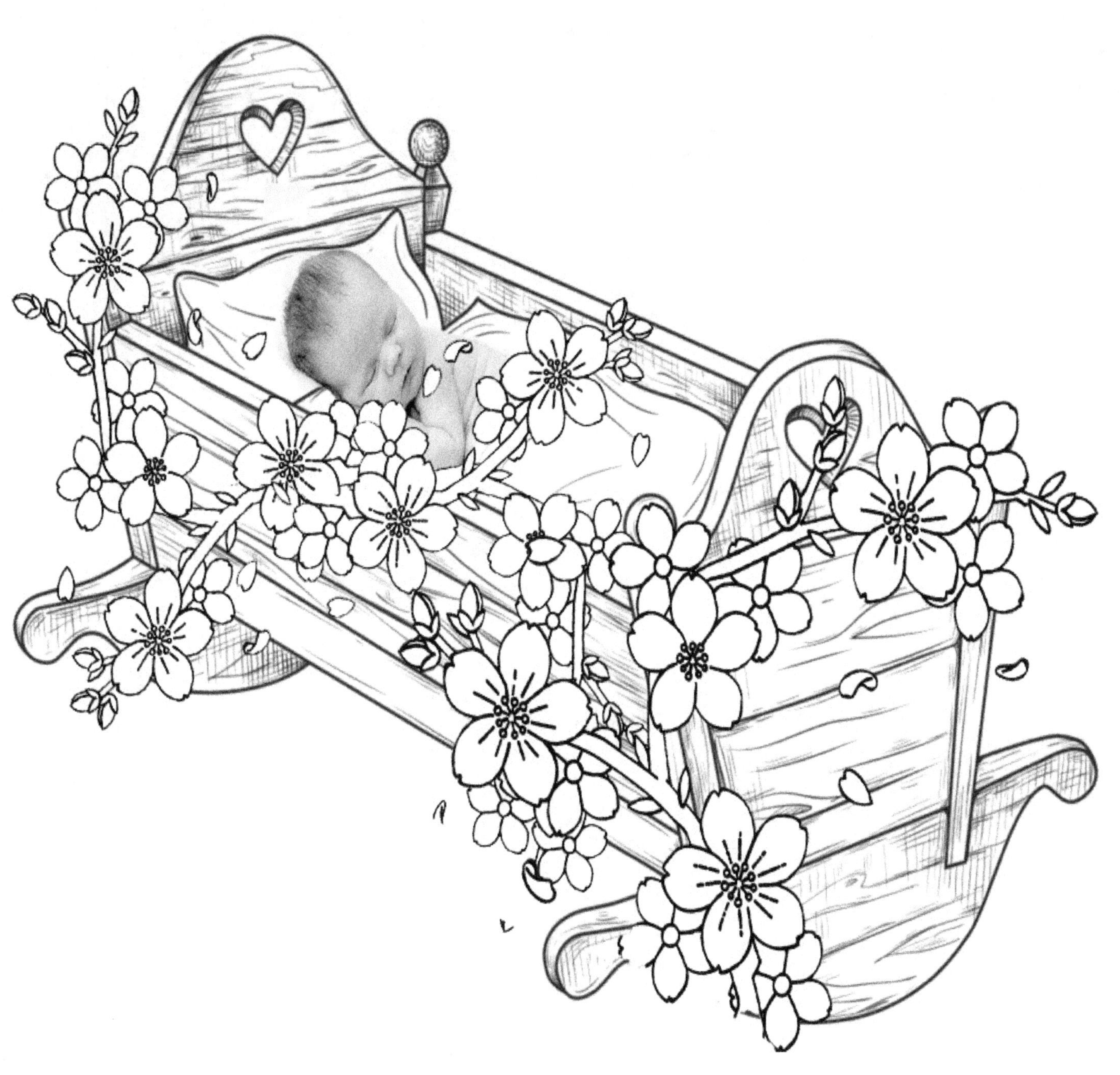

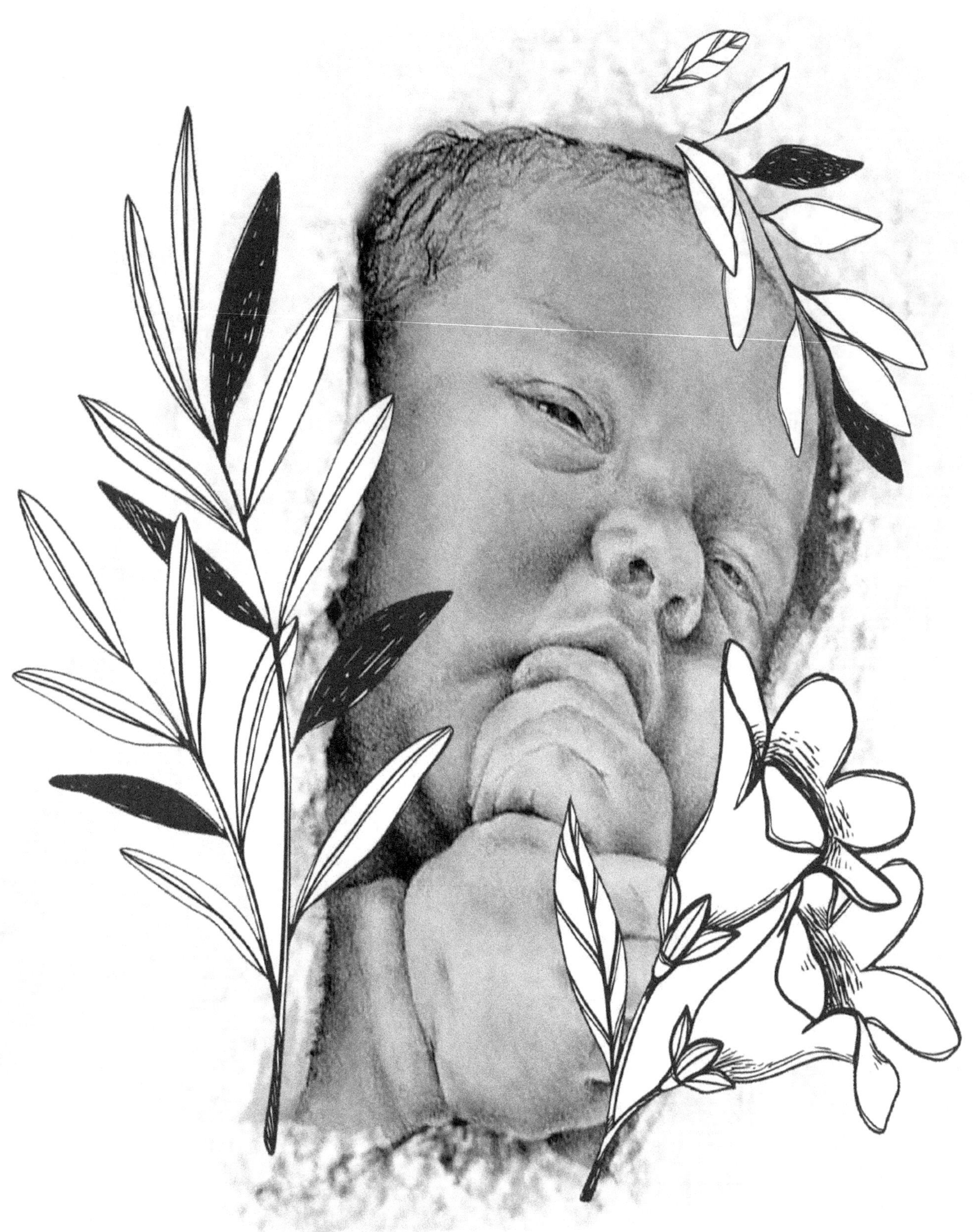

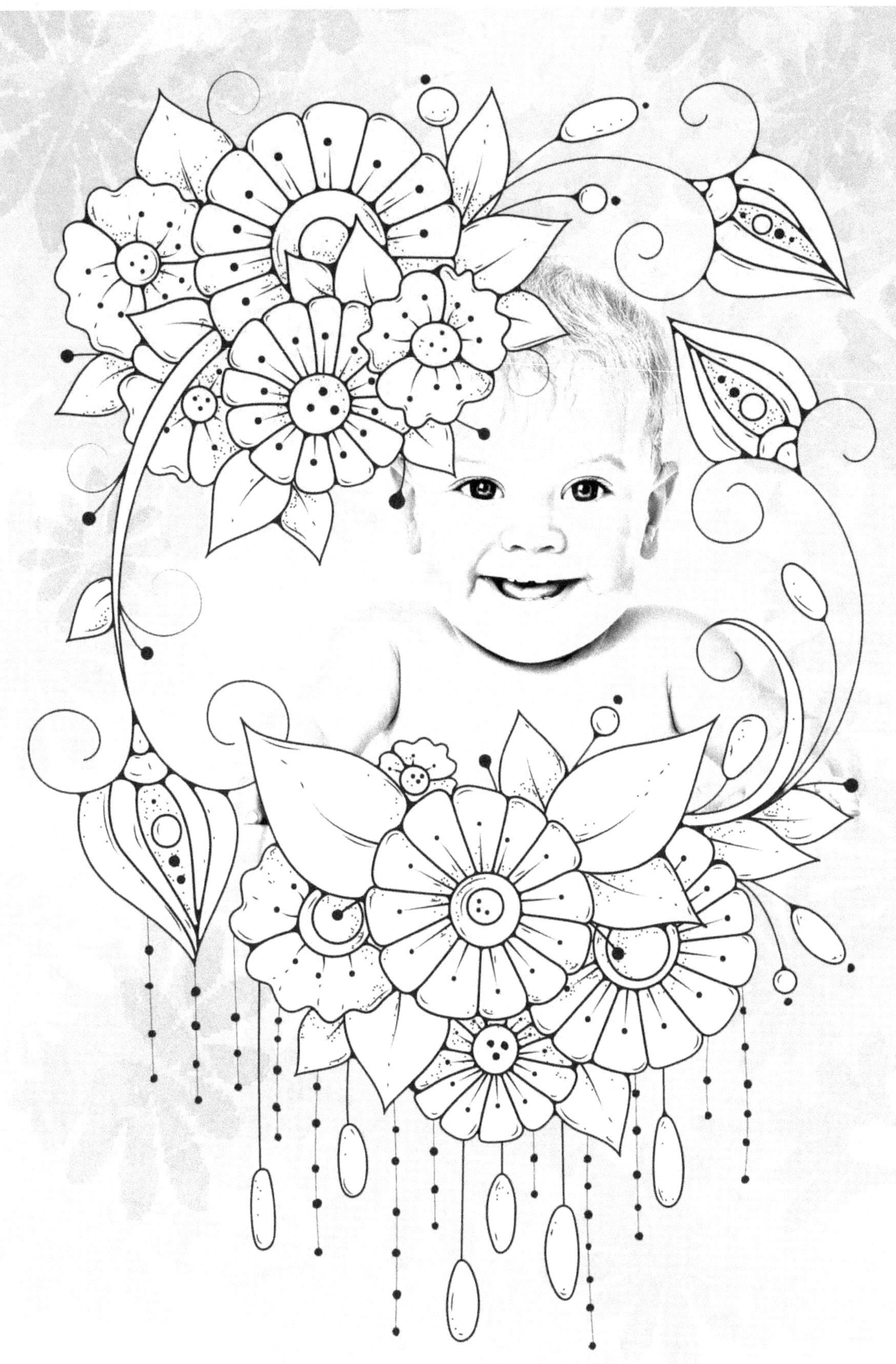

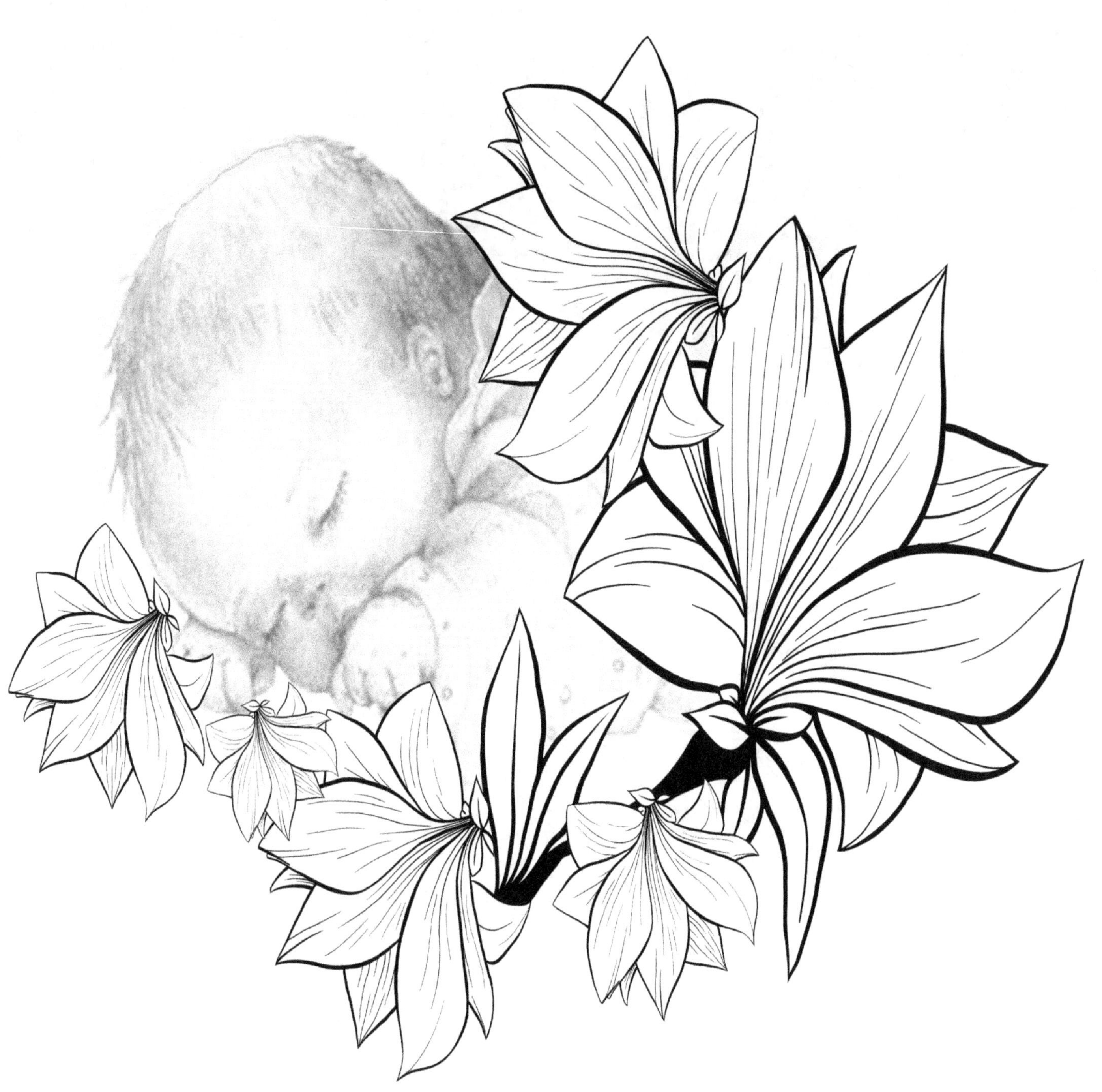

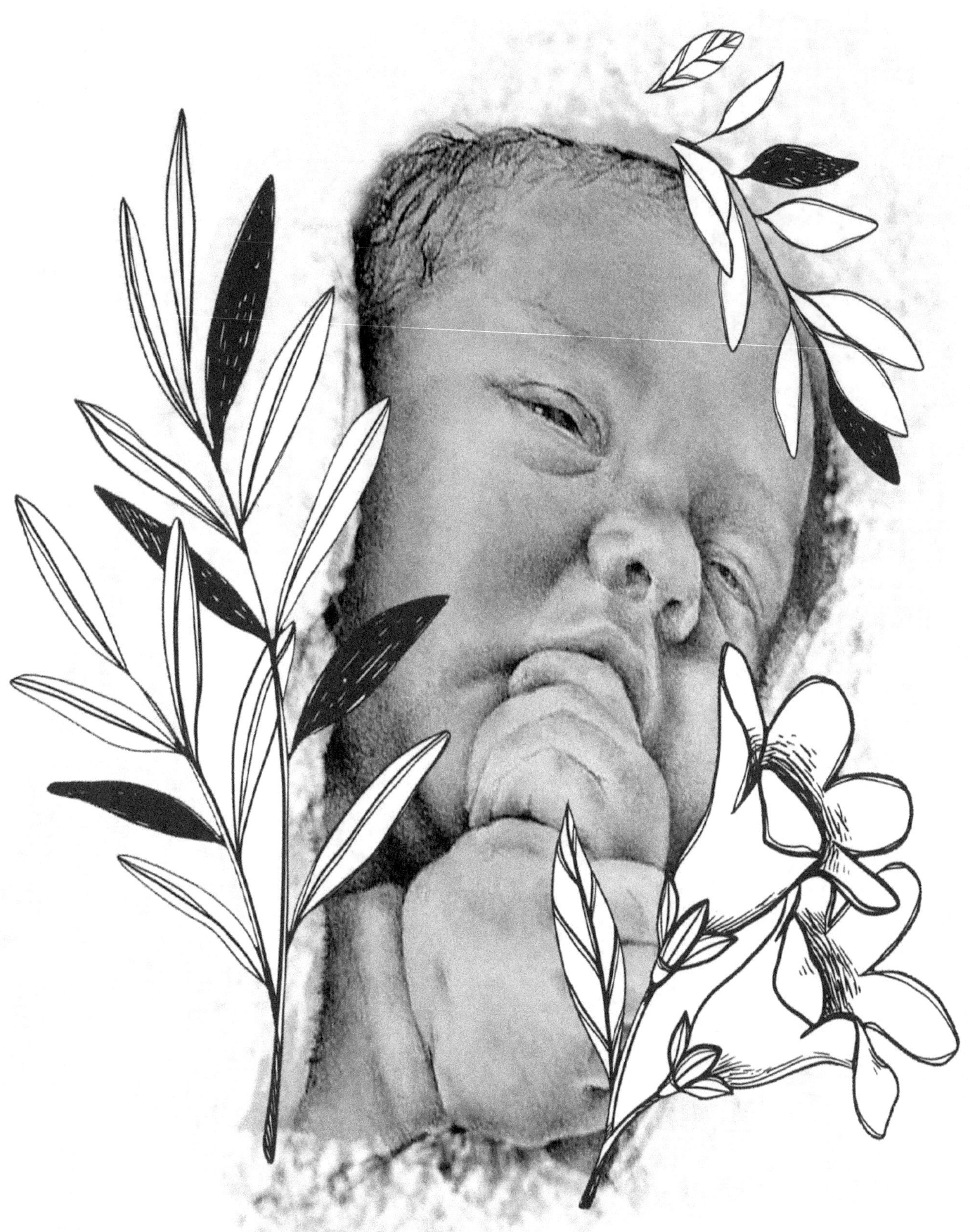

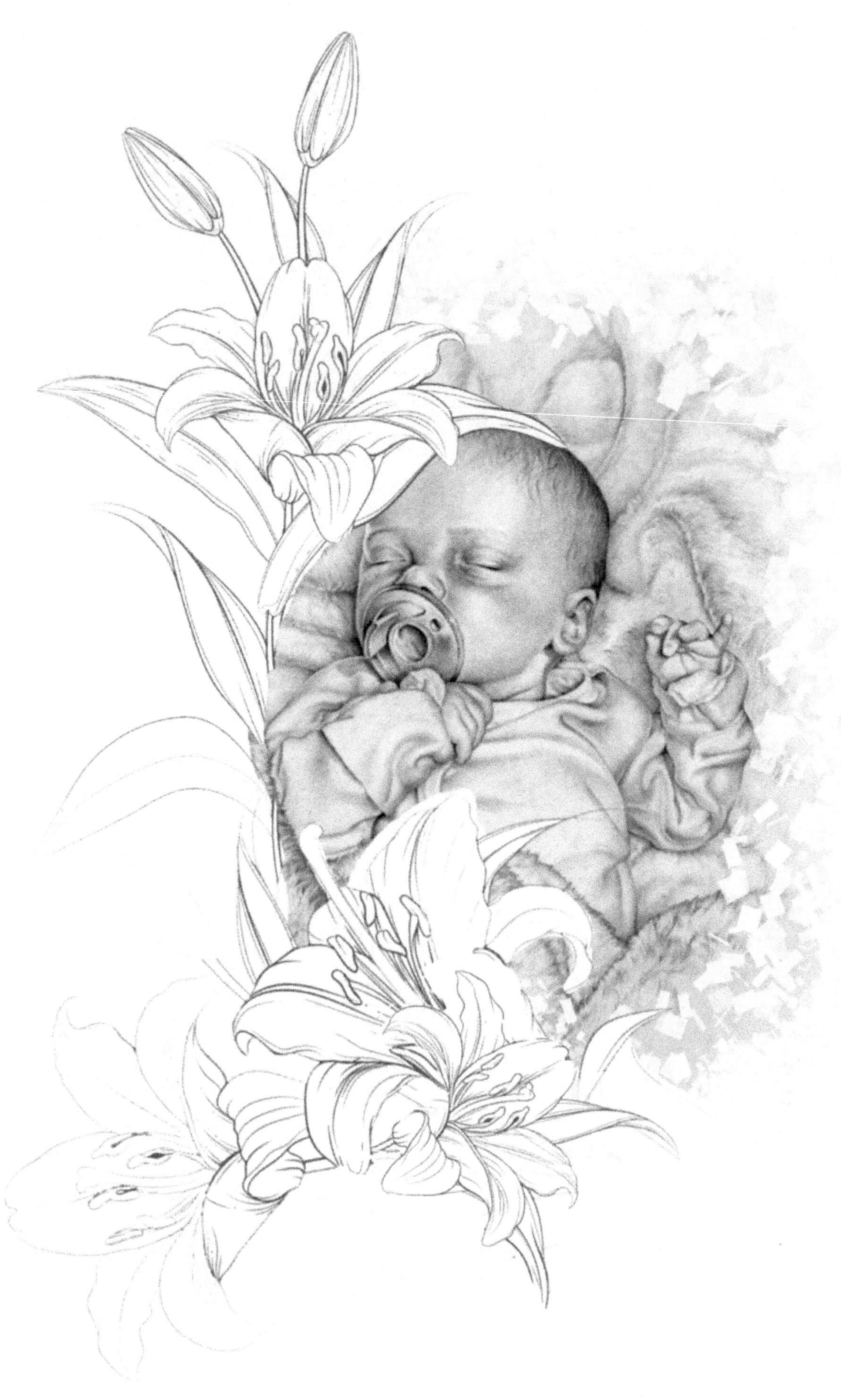

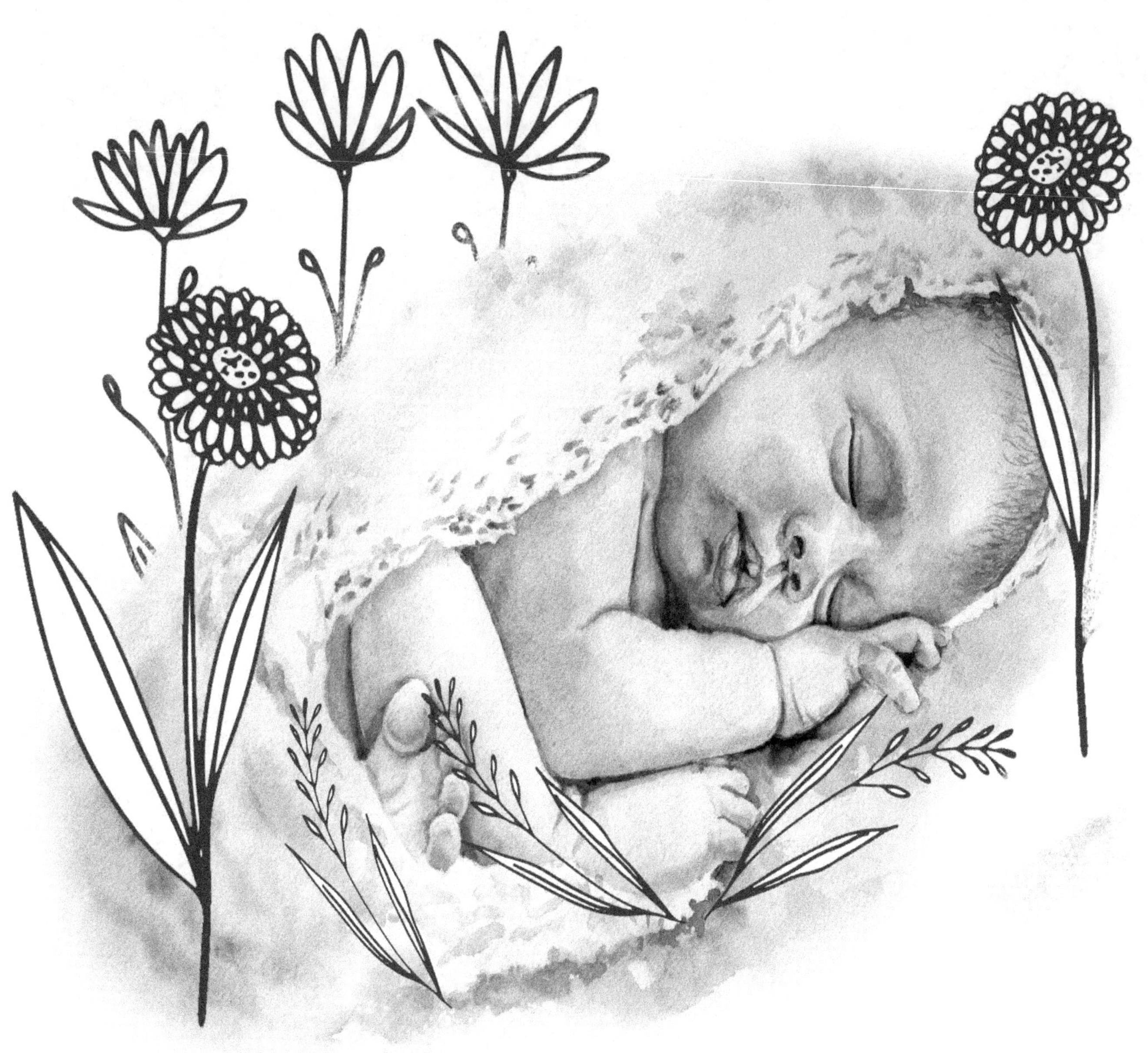

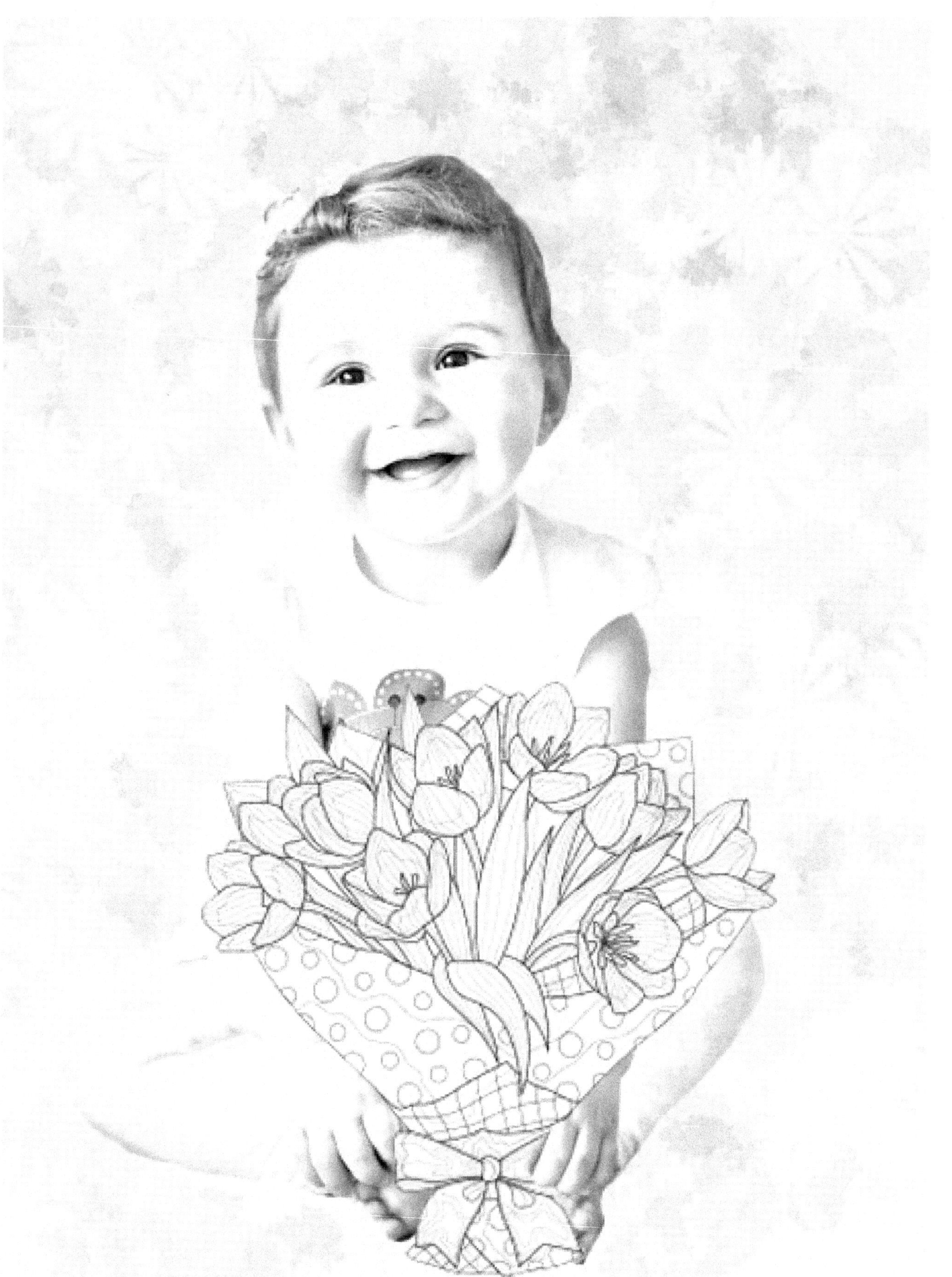

Also available in this Babies for Dementia Range

The Ocean · Babies and Flowers · Cupcakes · Tutti-Fruity

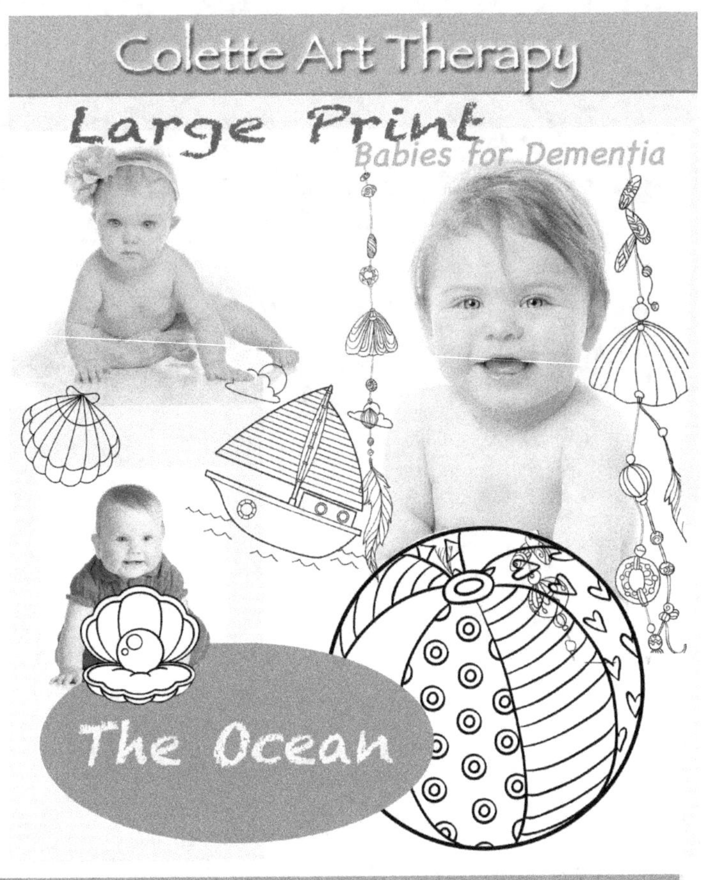

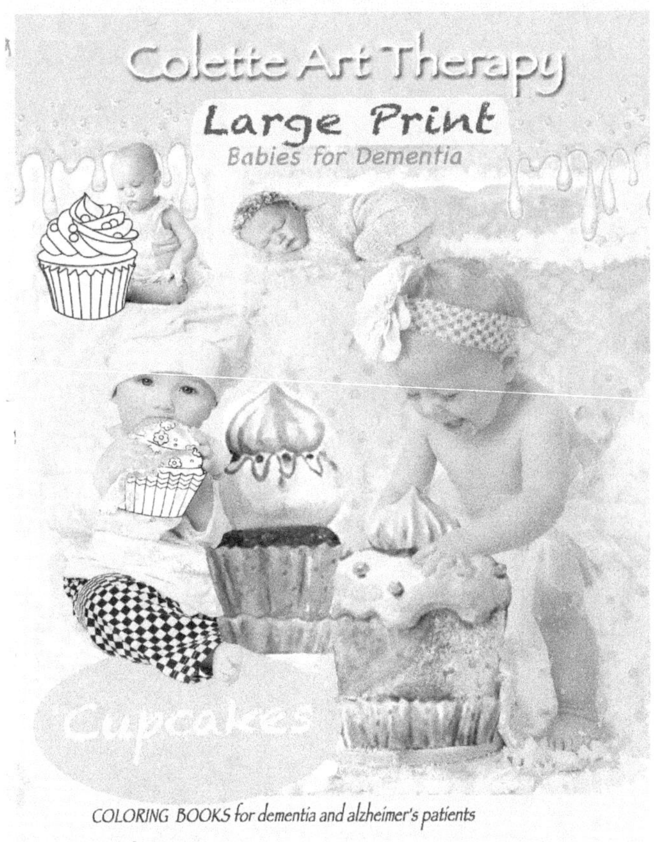

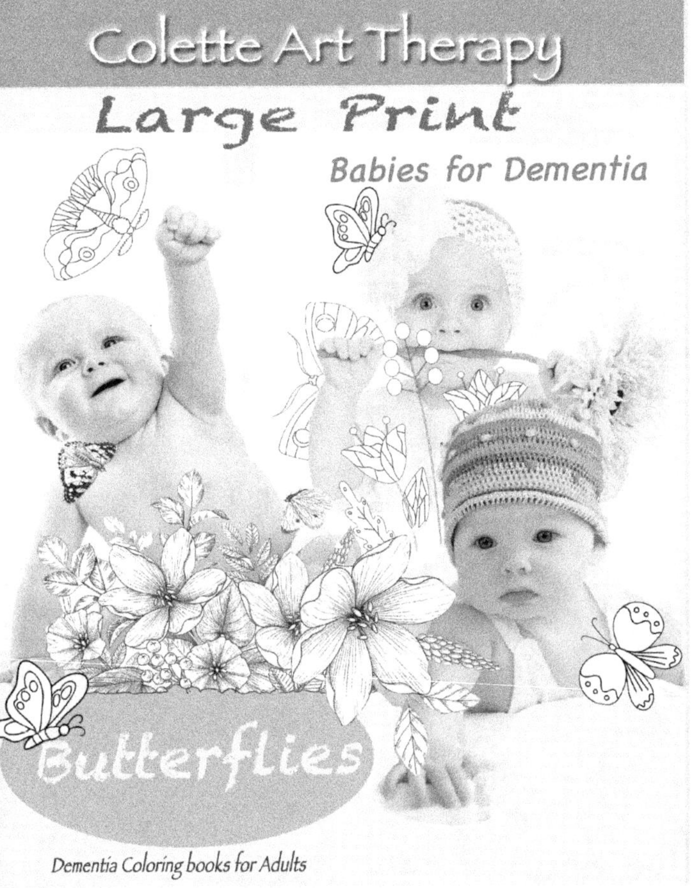

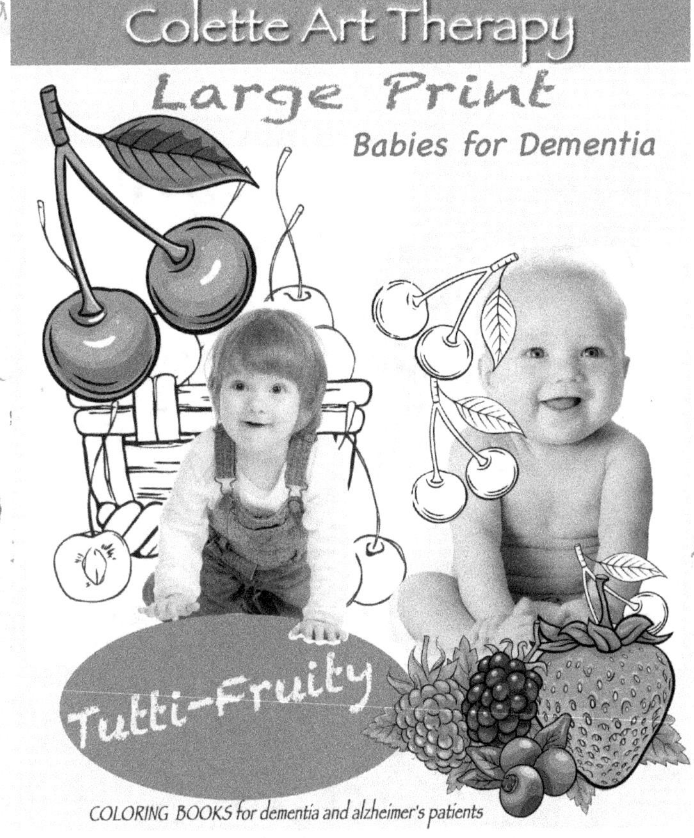

Also Available by Colette Art Therapy

Winter Wonderland

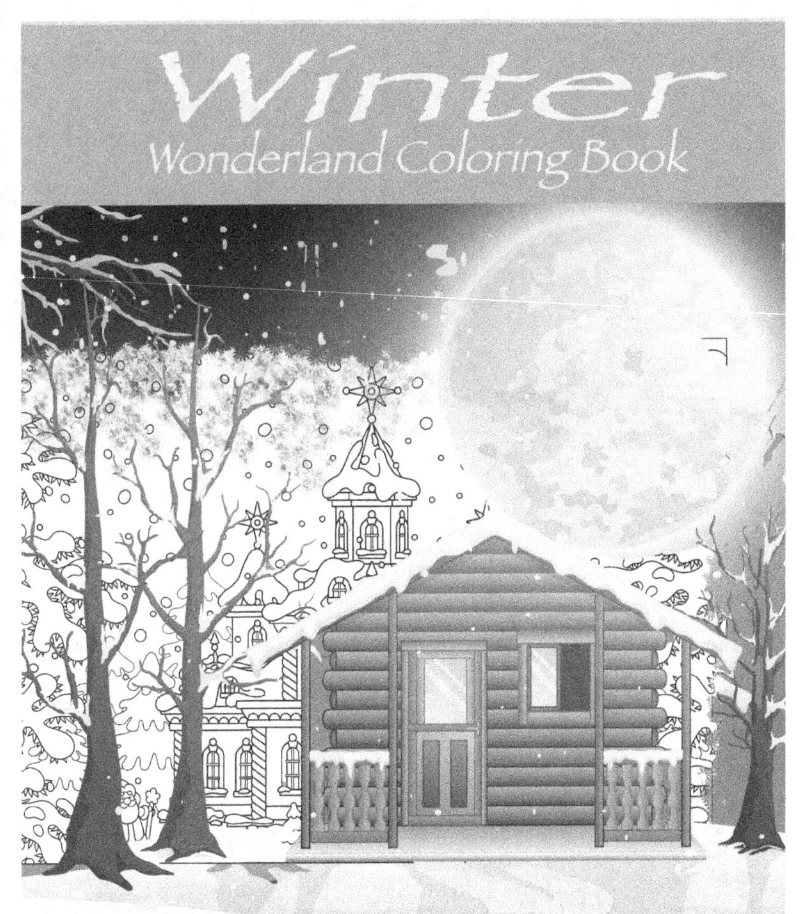

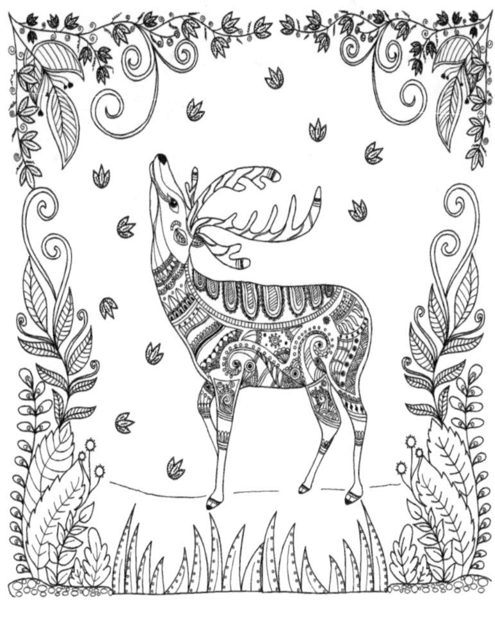

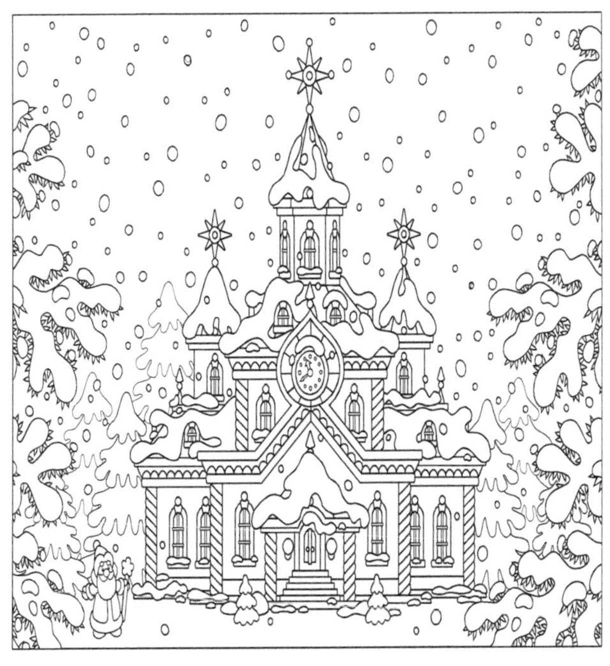

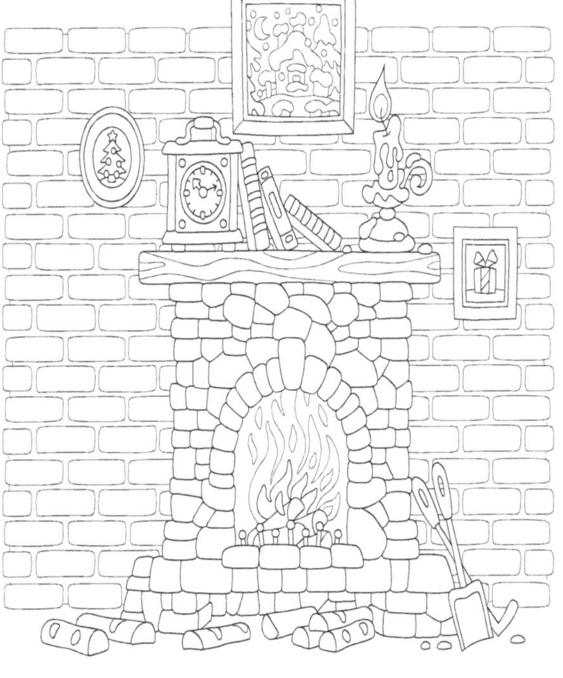

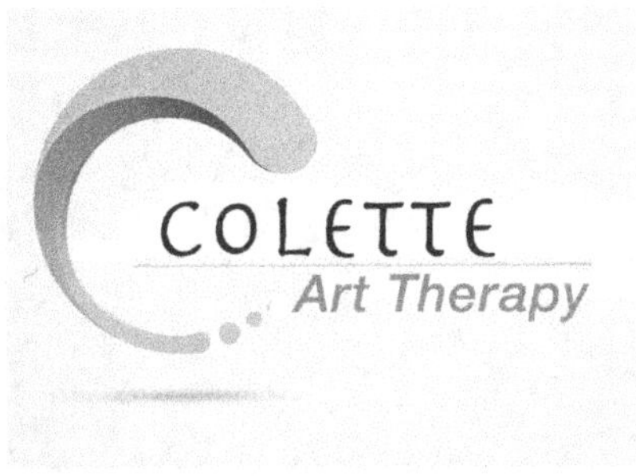

Share your coloured pictures
on Instagram,
Please tag us!

Colette.Art.Therapy

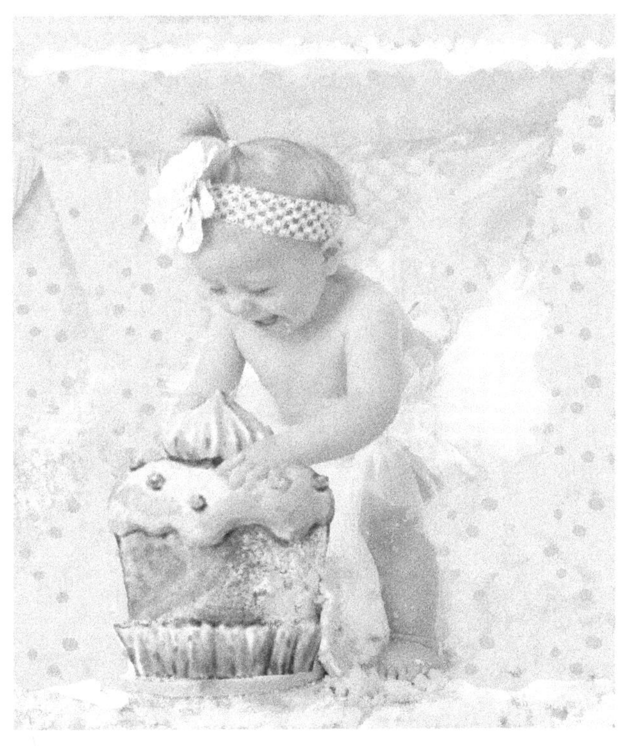

Www.ColetteArtTherapy.com